THIS BOOK IS LITERALLY JUST PICTURES OF CUTE DOGS THAT WILL BRING YOU JOY

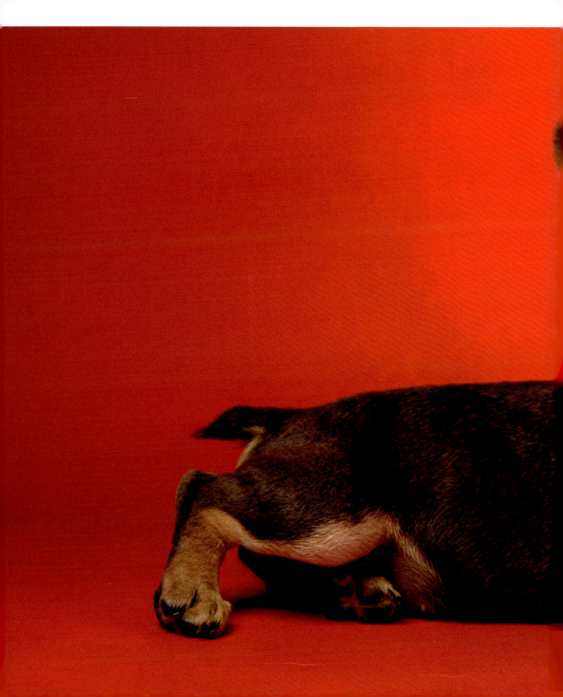

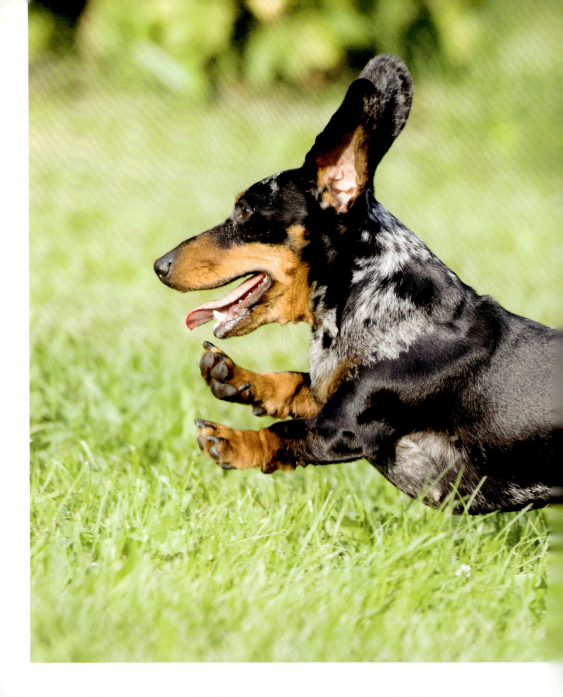

Published in 2025 by Smith Street Books
Naarm (Melbourne) | Australia
smithstreetbooks.com

Distributed outside of ANZ, North & Latin America by
Thames & Hudson Ltd., 6–24 Britannia Street, London, WC1X 9JD
thamesandhudson.com

EU Authorized Representative: Interart S.A.R.L.
19 rue Charles Auray, 93500 Pantin, Paris, France
productsafety@thameshudson.co.uk; www.interart.fr

ISBN: 978-1-9232-3935-7

All rights reserved. No part of this book may be reproduced or transmitted by any person or entity, in any form or means, electronic or mechanical, including photocopying, recording, scanning or by any storage and retrieval system, without the prior written permission of the publishers and copyright holders.

Smith Street Books respectfully acknowledges the Wurundjeri People of the Kulin Nation, who are the Traditional Owners of the land on which we work, and we pay our respects to their Elders past and present.

Copyright design © Smith Street Books

Publisher: Paul McNally
Design and layout: Hannah Koelmeyer
Cover photo: Eric Isselee/Shutterstock.com

Photo credits 32 iStock.com/RuthBlack. Shutterstock.com: front endpaper Seregraff; 4 Ermolaev Alexander; 14 Vitaly Titov; 15 Kashaeva Irina; 26 Masarik; 27 Photobox.ks; 30 michael_coelho; 31 Robert Moldvaji; 34 Javier Brosch; 36 Nikaletto; 38 Saley Yanny; 39 otsphoto; 42 OlgaOvcharenko; 44 otsphoto; 45 Jan Krava; 46 Natalia Fedosova; 48 BORINA OLGA; 50 xkunclova; 51 Svetlay; 52 KDdesign_photo_video; 54 S.Mac73; 56 Kwadrat; 57 MarBom; 58 Chendongshan; 68 Anna Averianova; 69 Natalia Fedosova; 78 otsphoto; 79 Ivanova N; 82 Liliya Kulianionak; 84 Callipso88; 88 BIGANDT.COM; 89 RavenaJuly; 92 tanya.asfir; 93 Anna Averianova; 94 Joel Everard; 96 Agus suriani; back endpaper Viola Ater

Printed & bound in China by C&C Offset Printing Co., Ltd.

Book 393

10 9 8 7 6 5 4 3 2 1